Don't just t

MW00648472

WHAT CAN I DEDUCT?
Record Keeping Tips to Minimize Your Taxes

Essential Oil Distributor Edition

WHAT CAN I DEDUCT?
Record Keeping Tips to Minimize Your Taxes

Essential Oil Distributor Edition

by
Dee Dee Stone

Table of Contents

My Checklist

☐ Open a business bank account.

☐ Open a business credit card. (Optional)

☐ Open a separate PayPal account. (See Chapter 3)

☑ Purchase a GREAT calendar.

☐ Build, buy, or download a mileage log.

☐ Create or download a sample log. (See Chapter 15)

☐ Decide if you want to save receipts on paper or electronically.

☐ Choose a method from Part II to keep track of income and expenses on a regular basis.

<u>Acknowledgement</u>

To those of you who coerced, I mean, encouraged me to write this book, thank you! I am grateful to have been given the opportunity to offer guidance to so many of you as you grow your businesses and seek financial freedom.

Introduction

Let's start with a brief introduction of what qualifies me to provide you with this tool. I graduated Magna Cum Laude from West Texas A & M University in 2001 with my bachelor's and master's degrees in accounting. I worked as an IRS auditor in the small business self-employed division in Dallas where I audited primarily sole proprietors filing Schedule C. I have owned my own bookkeeping and tax business since 2006, which also makes me self-employed. I also happen to be an essential oil distributor. Now that we got that out of the way, let's jump in!

Often, the greatest obstacles to running a business, have little to do with the business itself. Nearly every list you see with regard to why small businesses fail will have at least one financial reason for the failure. Many are started with too little money. Some just make poor spending choices. Rarely have I seen tax burden listed, but I have known many business owners who have considered closing up shop due to the complexity and burden of self-employment taxes.

You are in a unique industry. There is a low cost to get started. You need little or no money to share your story and offer alternative healthy solutions to others. The biggest obstacle to being a successful business owner and the one you have no way to avoid is taxes.

This book is meant to be a guide to get you on track with keeping up with your business income and expenses in a way that minimizes your tax liability. As an added bonus, you will be helping yourself out down the road if you are ever audited by your state or federal tax agencies.

So who is this book for? This book can be a useful guide to any essential oil distributor since most countries have similar accounting rules. More than anything this book is a guide to record keeping for your business. This book is a critical tool for every essential oil distributor in any state in the United States. I have been asked by several distributors, but what about State X? Most state tax laws are the same as the federal tax laws with regard to business deductions. There are minor exceptions that usually relate to how much depreciation you can write off for assets like furniture in a given year, but otherwise, the rules are pretty much the same and so are the record keeping strategies. This book is for those just getting started as well as those high ranking rock stars.

Before we get too far along, I want to give you a little basic Accounting 101 terminology.

Chart of Accounts - A chart of accounts (COA) is a complete listing of every category (or account) used for income, expenses, assets, and liabilities. For example, some accounts that might be used in this business are: Meals and Entertainment, Office Expenses, Postage, Telephone, and Travel. If those were the only categories/accounts, this would be your Chart of Accounts. I will use categories and accounts interchangeably throughout this book.

Cash Basis – this is a method of accounting that determines when you claim your income and expenses. Most businesses such as this operate on a cash basis.

Using the cash basis, income is taxed when it is received. This means commissions earned for December (20xx), but not paid until January (20xy) are taxed on your 20xy tax return.

Using the cash basis, expenses are **deductible when you pay them.** This means if you buy your convention ticket in June 20xx for convention in 20xy, you can write off the cost of the ticket as a business expense in 20xx. For credit card charges, the expense is deductible when you make the charge.

So if you charge your convention ticket in June 20xx for convention in 20xy, but you only make the minimum payment on your credit card for the remainder of 20xx, you still write off the full cost of the convention ticket on your 20xx tax return. This is because you do not write off the credit card payment itself, only the items you charge on the credit card. This is particularly important at year end. If you write a check or pay for a transaction with your credit or debit card on December 30' 20xx or 31' 20xx many times, those charges will not post to your account until January 20xy. Do not forget to account for these in 20xx!

Profit & Loss Statement – This is a report that summarizes your total income and expenses and shows you your "Net Income," which is the amount you really made and the amount you are taxed on. For example, your commissions are $25,000. You spend $1,000 on travel. You spend $250 on meals. You spend $2,000 on Team Development.

Your Profit & Loss Statement would look like this:

Profit & Loss Statement
For Period January 1, 20xx to December 31, 20xx

Total Income	$25,000	100%
Meals	$ 500	2%
Team Development	$ 2,000	8%
Travel	$ 1,500	6%
Total Expenses	$ 4,000	16%
Net Income	$21,000	84%

If you prepare these regularly (as the IRS would like you to do) you can compare numbers year-to-year or even month-to-month. You can start to anticipate slow months and better months and adjust your efforts accordingly. In this example, you can also see that you spent 8% of your income on Team Development. Maybe next year, you spend 20% on Team Development and you notice a 30% increase in commissions. This report can be a very useful tool as your business grows. It is a lot easier to get started compiling the data even before you understand it than it is to try to go back and figure it out when you want to look at the information.

PART I

Tools for Success

If you, implement each of the items in this section and you will have saved more than the cost of this book!

Chapter 1

Bank Account

The absolute best tool you can have for the financial side of your business is a separate checking account.

Some of you already want to stop reading. You are thinking to yourself either, "I don't make enough money yet to have a separate checking account." Or, "I can't keep up with another checking account." Just hear me out and I promise it will be worth it.

The first and best reason to have a separate checking account for your business is: THE IRS LOVES IT! In the event you are ever audited, the IRS will ask for your business bank statements and I guarantee if you are using your business account only for business, you will fare much better than those who are audited and are mixing business and personal expenses in one account.

The next best reason is it makes your life a lot easier to total up income and expenses. While you should be keeping track of income and expenses at least monthly, in real life, most of us don't. Be honest.

Many of you are scrambling at tax time to locate receipts and total up expenses just to get your return prepared on time. How much easier would it be if you could literally just go through 12 months of statements and total everything up? I often recommend clients print their statements, write the category for the expense next to the transaction, then go back and total expenses by category. This is so much quicker than adding up receipts or checking three personal accounts and four credit cards to come up with business expenses.

Guess what? The account does not even have to be a "business" checking account. You can simply open a separate personal account if that is what you prefer. This is probably much easier for those just starting out. The key is to have one checking account that you use exclusively for business.

QUICK TIP:

Most banks have a different color debit card for business accounts than they do for personal accounts. For many people, this makes it easier to be sure you are using the correct debit card when making purchases.

I recommend opening the account at the same bank you use for your other bank accounts. This makes transferring funds much easier. For example, especially if you are just starting out, you need to buy your convention ticket, but your commission check this month wasn't enough to cover the cost. You can just transfer the difference from your personal account into your "business" account and you are all set. This is much easier than having to write a check from your personal account and then depositing it at your "business" bank. Truth be told, very few would take the time to write that check and instead would just pay for the convention ticket from the personal account which would defeat the purpose of having a separate account.

I also recommend opening an account that has no monthly fee. Some banks charge a monthly fee, but will waive it if you have direct deposit or if you use your debit card at least 5 times per month.

Be sure to save your statement every month. You can either print them or save them electronically as a PDF. Remember, in the event you are ever audited, the IRS will want to see your business bank statements and many banks charge a fee if you have to request copies later.

How does this minimize my taxes?

1) *All your business expenses are in one place.*
   You remember those 37 trips you made to
   Walmart last year and now it's tax time and
   you don't know which were business and
   which were personal? Or what about that
   plane ticket to convention you charged on
   your Discover card but forgot about when
   you were totaling up your expenses?

2) *You get credit for every penny you spend!*
   Even if the transaction is only $1, if you
   always use your debit card rather than cash,
   it is much more likely the expense will be
   captured at tax time. Additionally, if you lose
   a receipt, you still have a record since it is on
   your bank statement, which means that
   expense still gets deducted.   (Now, just
   because you have a record doesn't mean you
   don't have to save receipts, but we will cover
   that a little later).

Chapter 2

Credit Cards

Unlike a checking account, you do not actually have to have a credit card. In fact, if you are a die-hard Dave Ramsey fan, you can totally skip this chapter. I would encourage you to at least skim it though.

Much like having a separate bank account, a separate credit card used just for business is a must IF you use credit cards. Why? Well, because the IRS LOVES IT! If you have a business (and you do), the IRS always wants to see that you have treated your business as a business by keeping your business and personal expenses separate. Aside from that, everything I said in Chapter 1 about the business checking account holds true for credit cards.

So why a whole chapter on credit cards? Well, to reiterate that everything for business should be separate and to cover a couple ways you can make your expenses work better for you that aren't necessarily tax related.

Your credit card, much like your checking account does not have to be a "business" credit card. It can simply be a separate personal card you use only for business. I recommend you choose a card with a low or no annual fee. I also recommend you pay the card off monthly to avoid interest charges and the accumulation of debt.

As you grow your essential oil business, there will be travel involved. Using a credit card to book travel has several advantages over a debit card. The biggest advantage is when you book a hotel or rental car, they generally preauthorize a lot less for incidentals or deposits. For example, when you go to rent a car, the rental car company will preauthorize an additional amount as a deposit. This amount varies by company. If you use a credit card, this deposit is generally less than if you use a debit card. Additionally, if you use a debit card, many rental car companies run a credit check before they will let you rent a car. A similar thing happens with hotels. Upon check in, even for prepaid rooms, you are required to give a credit or debit card for incidentals such as phone usage or mini-bar products. This amount is usually much less if you use a credit card. If you are on a tight budget, this can mean the difference in traveling for an event or staying home for many. Depending on the credit card, many automatically

QUICK TIP:

Don't use your accumulated rewards
(miles, hotel nights) to pay for
business expenses that you can write
off on your taxes. These can be used
to fund a personal vacation.

offer travel insurance if the travel is paid for with that
card. This includes rental car insurance.

Another advantage of using a credit card to make
your expenses work for you is cash back rewards!
Some of you may prefer miles and that is fine too. If
you charge every business expense on your
"business" credit card, you earn cash or miles for
every expense. As long as you pay it off monthly,
you are earning extra money.

Be sure to save your statement every month. You
can either print them or save them electronically as a
PDF. Remember, in the event you are ever audited,
the IRS may want to see your business credit card
statements and many companies charge a fee if you
have to request copies later.

How does this minimize my taxes?

1) *All your business expenses are in one place.*

2) *If you incur interest charges on a card used exclusively for business, your credit card interest is tax deductible as a business expense.*

3) *By paying for business expenses rather than using your rewards, you are preserving a tax deduction.* I can't tell you how many times I have had clients tell me they booked a flight or a hotel for a business trip using miles. Folks, while this saves you cash in that moment, unless you just can't go any other way, you are giving up a valuable tax deduction. There is no way to write off the cost of a trip you didn't pay for. This is also one of the draws for a cash rewards card rather than a miles card for me. You charge the flight or hotel on your credit card. You are earning cash back. You use accumulated cash rewards to pay the balance on the credit card statement, and you still get to write off the cost of that flight or hotel room.

Chapter 3

PayPal

I have a confession to make: I HATE PayPal. Sure, it's easy and convenient and you don't have to wait for people to mail you a check, but the financial reporting is horrendous! That being said, it is a popular way to send and receive funds, so I am going to cover the best way to track this for your business.

Remember how in both Chapters One and Two, I said the IRS LOVES IT when you keep your business and personal expenses separate? Yep, they love it when you do that with PayPal also. Some of you just let out a scream and it was not a scream of joy.

Obviously, my first recommendation is going to be to have a separate PayPal account just for your business. Much like the checking account and the credit card, you can just have two personal accounts. Maybe one is yours and one is your spouse's. Choose one and only use it for business. All those bulk buy deposits will go into the one for business and your birthday money from Grandma can go into the other.

I see some of your heads spinning right now as you think of all the separateness I am asking you to create. Good news! There's an oil for that.

If you don't think you can manage two separate PayPal accounts, I have a second recommendation. Keep your PayPal account balance at zero. What do I mean by that?

Let's say you do a bulk buy and when the shipment arrives, you take all the money in through PayPal. Immediately transfer the total amount you received in from those deposits to your business checking account. Likewise, any funds you receive for personal reasons, immediately transfer that amount to your personal checking account. When you want to pay an expense, simply choose which bank account to draft from depending on whether the expense is business or personal.

Just as with your business checking account and business credit card, be sure to save your statement every month. You can either print them or save them electronically as a PDF. Make sure your statements show the detailed activity.

How does this minimize my taxes?

1) *All expenses get included.* Many people forget to include the activity from their PayPal accounts when totaling up income and expenses for tax purposes or they assume it was a wash. The IRS wants you to include all deposits in income and all debits in expenses. I have had many clients over the years who have had much more in PayPal expenses than they realized.

Chapter 4

Calendar

A good calendar is the non-financial equivalent of a separate checking account. It is the best non-financial tool you can have. If you are only going to implement one thing from this book, make it a regularly, thoroughly completed calendar.

Why is a calendar more important than anything else?

A calendar that is kept up with day-to-day and is used to record appointments, notes, events, and even just scheduled tasks, can be used to rebuild pretty much anything. A complete calendar and a separate bank account can sometimes make the difference in a business and a hobby in the eyes of the IRS.

Think of your calendar as a diary of your business.

If you schedule a meeting, write on your calendar who it was with and where it was held. Now in the event you don't accurately keep up with mileage, you have a tool to rebuild mileage.

If you meet someone for coffee, lunch, dinner, etc, record that. The IRS does not require receipts for meals and entertainment expenses under $75 per occurrence, but they do require substantiation (evidence to support) in the form of who, what purpose, when, and where. If you jot these things on your calendar, BAM! It's done.

Record everything you do in your calendar. Record dates, times, and locations as well as the name of the person you are meeting with or event you are attending. Care calls - write them on the calendar. Peggy Sue in your downline had a baby and you sent a gift - write it down. You send out Team Development incentives to everyone who ranks up on the second Monday of every month - write it on your calendar. If you like to keep notes or you keep a pretty full schedule, get the daily page calendar so you have plenty of room to write.

Your calendar can be either paper or electronic. Personally, I prefer the Franklin Covey classic planner with daily pages. It is usually faster for me to jot something down than open up my app and type it in on my phone, and I don't have to worry about it crashing, getting a virus, or being stolen. The downside is I am lugging an extra item with me everywhere and there is no back up. Bottom line:

Choose whichever is going to be easiest for you to keep up with on a daily basis

How does this minimize my taxes?

1) *You can build substantiation.* The best example is of course, your mileage log. Whether you are calculating mileage to file your tax return (of course you aren't because you kept a mileage log!) or you are being audited and you either don't have or can't locate your mileage log, you can use your calendar and MapQuest to rebuild the number of miles you drove.

2) *You can "prove" expenses.* The most obvious category here is meals and entertainment, but you can also use your calendar to prove Gifts (assuming you keep good notes), Team Development costs, Class Material costs, etc. I will give you more detail on each of these categories in Chapter 13.

3) *You can demonstrate the profit motive of your business.* So, while this point only comes into play in the case of an audit and generally only if you have shown a loss for more than a couple years, your calendar can be used to prove you have a goal of making a profit in your business and that it is not just a hobby

(for which you cannot write off losses). If you can show the auditor the time spent (this is where the task list comes in) working on your business, it is far more likely you can prove you had a profit motive.

Chapter 5

Mileage Tracking

In order to deduct anything for business use of your vehicle, the IRS requires you to keep up with the miles you have driven. This holds true whether you are deducting actual expenses (gas, oil changes, etc) or standard mileage. I know it seems like a daunting task, but an accurate mileage log can save you hundreds, if not thousands, of dollars in taxes.

Gone are the days when the only way to track mileage was with a handy dandy notebook or one of those tiny little mileage books. In the ever evolving world of technology, keeping up with your mileage can be as easy as swiping left or right from your smart phone. So what information do you need and what is the best way to keep up with it?

Once per year, preferably as close to January 1st as possible, record your odometer reading. I would write this in your calendar. You will also need to do this if you sell or purchase a vehicle. For tax purposes, you need total mileage as well as miles driven for business, so if you write this down each year, total mileage is a breeze.

You need to save the receipts for repairs or maintenance on your vehicle. This is true whether you deduct actual expenses or standard mileage. Why? In the event of an audit, the IRS uses these receipts to verify the total miles driven for the year as well as for substantiation of the repairs and maintenance expense if you are deducting actual expenses. I recommend using the same garage, mechanic, or dealership for all maintenance (whenever possible) as it is usually pretty easy to go and get historical records if you ever need them. If you go to whatever shop you happen to pass by that day, it can make obtaining records more difficult if you misplace your originals.

You need to do this for each car you drive for business. If you have two vehicles at your home and you drive them interchangeably, you will need to keep separate records for each, including mileage logs.

The mileage record needs to show date, starting address, ending address, business purpose, and either number of miles driven or beginning and ending odometer reading.

Your mileage log is also a great place to keep up with tolls or parking fees you pay. I would highly recommend you log in to your toll tag account and print or save the monthly statement. Parking, especially in an area where you feed the meter (although many now accept credit cards), pay cash, or tip the valet, is an expense that adds up but is often overlooked when calculating expenses for tax purposes. Many times you do not get a receipt for parking, so excellent notes in your mileage log as you go can mean the difference in taking a deduction or not.

You can get vehicle mileage log books at most office supply stores for a couple bucks. You can keep this information on your calendar, which is what I do. Or, you can use a mileage tracking app such as MileIQ or TaxBot. If you use an app, just be sure to classify the trips as business or personal. If the app charges you a monthly fee, it's deductible!

If you are using an app, I recommend printing or saving to PDF a monthly report. There is no right or wrong way to keep track of this, so just like with the calendar, choose a method you can and will use consistently.

QUICK TIP:

If you are using an app that starts and stops automatically with movement, double check it regularly. I have yet to find one that doesn't glitch and short you several miles on longer trips.

How does this minimize my taxes?

1) *The post office is only five miles away!*

   Ten miles round trip, even just every other week adds up to 260 miles and a deduction of around $130 for the year, that's $33 dollars in tax savings, assuming a 25% tax rate (which includes self-employment tax). Now consider all those trips to the Dollar Store, Office Depot, or Wal-Mart plus meetings at Starbucks, classes you attend, or trips to the airport for conventions, retreats, and conferences. You just saved the cost of this book and can buy one for a friend!

Chapter 6

Sample Log

In spite of all the tax savings, some of you are ready to set this book on FIRE!!! Separate accounts, completed calendars, logging miles, and now SAMPLES! I promise, my intent is not to torture you.

So why do I recommend a sample log as a tool for success?

You already know the first reason is for tax purposes. While the best recommendation I can give regarding giving out samples is of course to have a separate bottle to give samples from than the bottle you use personally, this is not always practical. This leaves many wondering what exactly can you write off? You can check the Facebook groups or calculate for yourself, the price per drop. If you keep a sample log, you can then calculate EXACTLY what your deduction should be. This works to your advantage as many people underestimate how much they actually give away.

Your sample log needs to show the date, name and some type of contact information for the person you are providing the sample to, what oil you gave them as specifically as possible (number of drops), and WHY you gave it to them.

i.e. July 1, 20xx   Jane Smith   555-1212   20 drops lavender for itchy mosquito bites.

Each month when you are calculating your profit and loss information (or at tax time), you simply go through and total up what you spent on samples. Your sample log is really a great multi-purpose tool. Not only will it tell you how much you can write off, it can also be used as a marketing tool because you can follow up with the person you provided the sample to.

How does this minimize my taxes?

1) *You know exactly what you gave away!*

I have had many essential oil distributors tell me they just write off one out of every three bottles of a certain product or that they have only written off one bottle of any one oil per year simply because they didn't know how else to come up with what they spent on samples. If you keep a sample log, you may be surprised by the value of what you are giving away. This can mean a nice reduction in taxable income!

2) *That auditor won't need to think twice!*

In the event you are audited, the IRS will be impressed if you have this information. Not only will it substantiate what you are writing off, it also goes to show (if that is in question) this is truly a business and not just a hobby.

PART II

Methods for Success

The best method for recordkeeping is the one YOU
will use regularly, consistently, and completely.

Chapter 7

Paper

For centuries, business records have been kept on paper. Even today, though many of us make regular purchases online, the most common way we obtain proof of a transaction is using a paper record. Most stores and restaurants provide a paper receipt at the time of purchase. Only a couple places, such as Office Depot and Home Depot, have started giving you the choice of an email receipt.

Why might you choose paper recordkeeping as your method? Let me just tell you, the IRS loves paper. They understand paper. It doesn't take them extra weeks of training to know how to review your records. It is by far the simplest method of record keeping we have available.

If you are going to keep all your records on paper, I recommend getting an accordion file or photo storage type box with multiple dividers.

> Resist the urge to organize your
> receipts by month. Label your
> dividers by CATEGORY!

This makes it much easier, in the event you skipped Part One and are still adding up receipts just in time for your tax filing, to go through and total up expenses by category. You can check the Appendix at the end of this book for a sample chart of accounts to help get you started.

Although paper is the simplest method of keeping up with your records, there are some pitfalls to doing it old school. First, some of your receipts will fade. While it is true that if you can't read them neither can the IRS, if you are trying to read them to calculate deductions, that might be a problem, especially if you paid cash. Paper receipts also take up space. Maybe you don't have many, but year after year, that is a lot of accumulation. Another downside to paper is you can only access your records if you are in the same physical location as your documents. You have no backup.

Paper recordkeeping exclusively does not lend itself well to easily preparing Profit & Loss statements or comparison reporting such as year-to-date, prior year, or even percentage of expenses. These are things you will want to see when you start reaching higher ranks and your income level begins to skyrocket!

One last thing you want to consider is, will this method grow with me to the highest rank I wish to achieve?

.

Chapter 8

Excel

While not as old as paper, Excel is the next oldest method of record keeping, especially for those of us who grew up on paper and cut our teeth on spreadsheets when computers first became mainstream.

Excel does not alleviate the need to store your paper receipts, but it sure is handy for totaling up expenses. If you keep consistent records in Excel, by category, tax time should just be a summary printout away. Excel also allows you to build a Profit & Loss statement and look at comparative reports.

The easiest way to track income and expenses in Excel is to simply enter them line by line. You can enter date, place, amount, category, and business purpose. Later you can sort and filter however you choose to get your totals or even build reports using formulas and tables.

Since you still need to keep your paper receipts, just

as in the last chapter, I recommend using an accordion file or photo storage type box organized by category rather than by month.

You also have the option of scanning your receipts and saving them electronically. If you do this, I recommend creating a new folder each year. I name my receipts as follows:

Best Buy 20xx 06 30

This makes finding receipts much easier later. You can go a step further if you like and name them by category first, such as Office Expense Best Buy 20xx 06 30. I do not use this method as sometimes you have multiple categories of expenses on one receipt and that can get a bit confusing.

While Excel is easier to use for reporting purposes than paper, it is also subject to a great deal of human error. The most common errors are data entry and formulas. What if you have more than 100 lines of one expense and you just keep typing through the box with the formula? Or you add lines and forget to update your formula? These simple mistakes cost you tax dollars. Always double check!

Anytime you are using your computer for business data, or even personal data for that matter, you need a method to back up your information. It is unlikely someone is going to break into your home and steal boxes of receipts, but I have known several people who have had their laptop or iPad stolen. Computers can also be hacked or get viruses. The IRS will take this excuse about as well as your high school English teacher would have accepted the dog ate your homework. If Excel or scanned receipts is your preferred method for success, make sure you use a good back up like iCloud, Carbonite, or Dropbox. Personally, I back up my computer to Carbonite and copy important files to Dropbox.

Chapter 9

Apps

Welcome to the 21st century, where there is literally an app for just about everything!

By far, the easiest way to keep up with income and expenses for those non-accountant types who hate paper and love having everything right at their fingertips is the smartphone app.

There are likely many different apps on the market for this very purpose, but the one I have had the most experience and success with is TaxBot. Not only can you can choose to sync the app with your bank account and have all your transactions imported in, you can also snap pictures of your receipts and do away with all the paper clutter!

The app makes recordkeeping easy through the use of automatic downloads and a few swipes of your finger. Import your transactions straight from your bank every week. Categorize your income and expenses as either business or personal (hopefully all business since you have separate accounts for everything now) and by category such as Office Expense or Meals and Entertainment. Snap a picture of your receipt to go with the transaction and you are done! Be sure to save your statement every month. You can either print them or save them electronically as a PDF.

Apps also have the added advantage of having an automatic backup. If you lose your phone or it is otherwise impaired or inaccessible, since your data is stored with the app company, you can log in and access from anywhere.

Any app (or system) is only as good as the data that goes in. As long as you get all the data entered into the app, you can see a pretty nice picture of how your business is doing. If you use the same app to track your mileage, you don't even have extra work to figure out your mileage deduction.

While there are many advantages to using an app, I have to say the biggest disadvantage is generally the monthly fee. The fee is deductible as a business expense and if you use the app regularly and consistently, the benefit will far outweigh the cost.

Another potential disadvantage is making sure you keep your billing method up to date so you don't lose your data. I have known a few people who have had issues when their credit card information changed. For example, your credit card was replaced and you forgot to update the payment information for your subscription. Some companies have been known to delete your data after as short a period as one week.

Overall, if you had no preference and I had to recommend one method, this is the method.

Chapter 10

Software

For those of you who love numbers, you can always use a full blown software program such as Quicken or QuickBooks.

Quicken is really more of a home use software and is more limited in its business reporting capabilities, while QuickBooks is one of the best small business accounting software programs on the market. Both programs are relatively user friendly and offered in an online version allowing you access from anywhere.

Both programs will link with most bank and credit card accounts for automatic download. You do still have to classify each transaction by income or expense account. These programs offer profit and loss statements at the click of a button, as well as comparison reporting and charts and graphs.

Just as with Excel, you still have to have a method to keep up with receipts if you are using a software program. I recommend using an accordion file or photo storage type box organized by category rather than by month. You also have the option of scanning your receipts and saving them electronically.

The biggest disadvantage to one of these programs is the cost. While it is true you can use the same program year after year without upgrading, the upfront cost makes these programs cost prohibitive for some.

These programs are generally geared toward serious numbers people as compared to the other methods we have covered. All too often I have clients who have purchased QuickBooks and spent literally hundreds of dollars, but then never use it. If numbers aren't your thing, I do not recommend this method.

Chapter 11

Hire a Pro

For some of you, there is no method simple enough to make you want to do this on your own. If you are one of these people, do yourself a favor: HIRE A PRO!

You don't have to spend thousands of dollars. In fact, if you follow everything I said in chapter one, a good professional bookkeeper should only cost you a few hundred dollars a year, tops. Obviously the less organized you are, the more it will cost. This is a cost you can write off, but it is also a cost you can control.

Maybe you don't feel you can afford to hire someone yet. You can also choose a lower cost option and have a high school or college student enter the information into the program or app of your choice. Just remember, you usually get what you pay for and many times students (unless they are beyond first year accounting students) do not know how to properly categorize expenses.

PART III

What Can I Deduct?

Chapter 12

Income

Why are we starting the section on what you can deduct with income? Because it is important to know the proper way to report your income as well as your expenses.

The Internal Revenue Code section 61(a) defines income as "gross income means all income from whatever source derived, including (but not limited to) the following items:

Compensation for services, including fees, commissions, fringe benefits, and similar items; Gross income derived from business; Gains derived from dealings in property; Interest; Rents; Royalties; Dividends; Alimony and separate maintenance payments; Annuities; Income from life insurance and endowment contracts; Pensions; Income from discharge of indebtedness; Distributive share of partnership gross income; Income in respect of a decedent; and Income from an interest in an estate or trust."

To summarize this in English, the IRS pretty much believes that all deposits you can't prove are not income, are income.

Why is this important?

Many of you are hosting make and takes, offering classes or organizing events, and even making bulk purchases for which you are receiving money. In your mind, this money may all just be considered a wash, offsetting the cost. After all, if you buy 100 books for $10 each and then sell them for $10 each, you haven't actually made any money. I agree. However…. the IRS expects to see the receipt of that money listed as income. You then deduct the amount you paid for the expenses on the appropriate line. So in this example, you have $100 in income and $100 in Bulk Buy Purchases expense.

The one exception to including all deposits as income is refunds. Refunds offset whatever the expense was for. For example, let's say you paid $250 for your hotel for convention but then found out you were not going to be able to make it. The expense would originally have been deducted under Travel and for the year you have total travel expenses of $1,000. The refund will cancel out $250 for travel so your total deduction for Travel is now $750.

In the event you are ever audited and the IRS reviews your bank statements, one of the first things they do is look at your total deposits per the bank and compare that to the total income reported for your business on your tax return. If these numbers match, great! If they do not, the IRS will attempt to make you include all unaccounted for deposits as income. This is another great reason to a) have a separate bank account and b) report income on the appropriate line.

What records do you need to keep for income?

Keep your monthly commission statement. You can either print this or save it to PDF. Not only does this show a record of your commission income, it also shows the maintenance fee you are charged, which is a deduction.

If you are charging for anything, make and takes, classes, events; the best thing to do for yourself and anyone who attends and might need a receipt for their records is to issue them a sales receipt. You can get an inexpensive receipt book at most office supply stores. Short of that, have a sign in sheet that includes the date, the name of the event, each attendee's name, and the price they paid. The same is true for bulk buys. If you aren't able to issue receipts, at least have a sheet with the date, the publication or product you purchased, the quantity you bought, the name of each person who is buying from you, the quantity of items they bought from you, and how much they paid you. You don't have to use paper, you can do this in Excel or a note app as well.

REMEMBER:

When in doubt, the IRS will side in their own favor so make sure you keep excellent records!

Chapter 13

Expenses

You've made it! You are finally to the chapter that tells you what you can deduct!

The Internal Revenue Service Publication 535 states "a business expense must be both ordinary and necessary. An ordinary expense is one that is common and accepted in your industry. A necessary expense is one that is helpful and appropriate for your trade or business. An expense does not have to be indispensable to be considered necessary.

Even though an expense may be ordinary and necessary, you may not be allowed to deduct the expense in the year you paid or incurred it. In some cases you may not be allowed to deduct the expense at all. Therefore, it is important to distinguish usual business expenses from expenses that include the following.

- The expenses used to figure cost of goods sold.
- Capital expenses.
- Personal expenses."

As you can see, the tax code leaves much to interpretation when it comes to expenses. In the paragraphs that follow, I will give you expense items and descriptions where necessary. Please note this is not an all-inclusive list nor will every expense item apply to every distributor. When in doubt, please consult your own tax professional as that person will be able to guide you best in your own personal situation.

If ever you have an expense you feel may be questioned, make a note of the details such as who you were with, purpose it was for, etc on the receipt. I also recommend adding a detailed note on your calendar.

The expense items will follow in alphabetical order. If there is an expense category here you do not see on your tax form, don't panic. Every tax form (at least for business reporting) has an Other Expense line. You will simply deduct these there. Once you have determined which expense categories you use, I recommend you label your file for your receipts accordingly, if you are keeping paper receipts.

Advertising - this category generally becomes a one size fits all where people put everything they don't know how to classify. I caution against this as it also makes it one of the most audited expense categories on any business tax return. Examples of items that can be appropriately included in advertising are: Facebook ads to promote your business and/or classes, advertisements to promote a booth at trade shows or other events. Be sure to keep receipts!

Auto Expenses – we covered the mileage log in Chapter 5. This is the category where all things auto related will go on your tax return. There are two methods of deducting auto expenses: Standard Mileage and Actual Expenses. Both are deducted here.

Standard Mileage includes the number of business miles driven multiplied by the standard mileage rate as set by the IRS each year. It also includes amounts paid for parking and tolls, as well as a percentage of the interest paid on your auto loan if you are financing your vehicle. For standard mileage, you should keep a mileage log, repair and maintenance receipts, parking and toll receipts and statements, and if you are paying on an auto loan, your auto loan statements that show the interest paid.

Actual Expenses include depreciation, gas, repairs and maintenance, parking and tolls, registration, tires, car washes, and insurance. If you are financing your vehicle, it includes a percentage of the interest on the loan. If you lease your vehicle, it also includes a portion of the lease payment. For actual expenses, you should keep a mileage log. You will need the bill of sale from the purchase of your vehicle for the depreciation. You should also keep receipts and statements for gas, repairs and maintenance, parking and tolls, registration, tires, car washes, and your auto insurance. If you are paying on an auto loan, you should keep your auto loan statements that show the interest paid and if you are leasing, you should keep the statements that show your monthly lease payment. As you can see, actual expenses require a lot more record keeping!

Bank Fees – if you have a business bank account, you can deduct any monthly service charges, overdraft fees, ATM withdrawal fees, wire transfer fees, and foreign transaction fees. Your bank statement is your receipt!

Bulk Buy Purchases – you can include anything you purchase in bulk here. Maybe you got a great deal on some conference tickets if you bought ten and your downline members are reimbursing you. The reimbursement is income. The cost of the tickets that are not your own go here. The same goes for books, diffusers, oils, or anything else you buy that you will be reimbursed for. Keep receipts and keep a log of who reimburses you, the amount, the product, and the date!

Class Materials – anything you purchase to host a class (that is reasonable and necessary) should be deducted here. This includes booklets or pamphlets you may provide, oils, sample bottles, and food. This is the one and only place you can take a 100% deduction for food costs. This means if you bake brownies for the whole class so you can demonstrate the use of peppermint oil in the brownies and make lemonade to demonstrate the use of lemon oil in the lemonade, you can write off the cost of all the ingredients as class materials. If you host a class at a restaurant or have food catered for a class, you can write off the full cost. I recommend taking photos of classes you host and be sure to capture the refreshments provided as well. Keep all receipts, including those for the food and an attendance sheet! Document this class on your calendar!

Computer & Internet – all things computer go here, EXCEPT for your computer. This is where you write off the cost of software such as QuickBooks, Dropbox or antivirus software. You can include monthly subscription fees here for apps such as TaxBot and Oily Tools. You can also include repairs for your computer here. Please note for computer repairs, if you only use your computer 50% for business, you can only take 50% of the repair cost. Keep receipts! If you have a monthly subscription with a recurring charge, your bank statement can serve as the receipt. Home internet also goes here. I would not recommend deducting more than 50% of the cost for Internet for your business. I would also be careful to include only the Internet portion if your bill includes the Internet as part of a bundled package with your cable television, which is not generally deductible. Save your monthly bill!

Dues & Subscriptions – you can include monthly recurring app and software fees here, instead of in Computers & Internet, if you prefer. This category is also where you would include dues for any professional associations you may belong to and magazine subscriptions related to your business.

Gifts – the IRS gift limit is $25 per person per year. This means you need to be extra mindful of what goes in this category. I reserve this account for actual gifts for things such as birthdays, graduations, new babies, etc. If you send something out to a team member related to their business performance, such as when they reach the next rank, I recommend classifying that as Team Development. Keep receipts with the name and reason for the gift!

Interest – you can deduct interest expenses for business loans and business credit cards. This means if you took out a business loan in the business name or if you have a personal loan, but can definitively prove you used all the money borrowed for your business, you can deduct the interest on that loan as a business expense. The same holds true with credit card charges. This is another excellent reason to designate one card for business use only. Keep your monthly statements as your receipt!

Legal and Professional Fees – you can deduct fees you pay to professionals if the fees are related to your business. These fees include those for accountants, lawyers, and tax professionals. Technically speaking, you cannot deduct the full cost of your tax preparation fees here if you are a sole proprietor since your personal tax return is required whether you have a business or not. Speak to your tax professional about breaking the invoice out to show time spent on the business portion of the return separately. Keep the invoices you receive as your receipt!

Maintenance Fees – these are the fees deducted from your commission. Keep your monthly commission statements as your receipt!

Meals and Entertainment – ALL meals go here! This includes meals when you are traveling, dining with a prospective member, or meeting with someone who is already a member of your down line. If you pay for food and it is not as described under Class Materials, it goes in this category. This is important because Meals and Entertainment are only deducted at a rate of 50%. All entertainment goes here as well. The IRS allows for entertainment that occurs immediately before or immediately after a business meeting/event to be. Let's say you attend convention and after your last session, you have dinner with a couple members of your downline and then you all go to the theatre. This can be considered a business entertainment expense because the activity occurred immediately after your business meeting. This is a very commonly abused and frequently audited category. The IRS does not require you to keep receipts for any meal or entertainment cost that is LESS than $75 per occurrence. You are however required to keep the who, what purpose, when, and

63

where. Your calendar is the best place to keep this information!

Merchant Fees – this category includes fees you are charged by Amazon, E-Bay, Etsy, PayPal, and any merchant services provider you use to accept credit cards such as Shopify or Square. You should be able to print or save to PDF monthly statements from each of these as your receipt!

Office Furniture and Equipment – this category is a bit tricky for some. If you buy a desk, a printer, a computer, etc that can be used year after year, it goes here. Your tax professional will let you know if it can be written off in its entirety in the year it is purchased or if it needs to be depreciated over time. A good general rule is if the cost per item is greater than $500, it needs to be listed as a depreciable item and then depreciated. Keep receipts!

Office Expenses – this category is where you will write off your paper, printer cartridges, paper clips, pens, markers, etc. I recommend if you purchase these items from an office supply store, you get a rewards card. I always buy office supplies at Office Depot. I also recycle my printer ink cartridges there. In any given year, I earn $200 - $300 in rewards that can be used for school supplies for my daughter, SD cards for my camera when I travel on vacation, etc. Just as with your miles and cash back rewards, use the rewards for personal expenses if you can or even to buy extra school supplies to donate to the school, church, or community members who may need a hand up! Keep receipts!

Postage – this one is pretty self-explanatory! Keep receipts!

Professional Development – this category is for all the expenses you incur to further your knowledge and growth in your business. If you attend classes about oils, network marketing, being an entrepreneur, they all go here. This is also where you put tickets for conferences and seminars you attend such as convention or Oola. Love to read? Books you purchase to increase your knowledge about oils, business, and yes, even this book, all go here as well. I caution you to be mindful of the categories you use on your tax return. I see many people include these under an expense category on their tax return called Education. The problem with this is education is generally speaking not a deductible business expense and you are generally allowed to deduct only qualified education expenses (such as college tuition) as Tuition and Fees on Form 1040 or claim an education credit. Sometimes, just the wording makes a difference in the level of scrutiny. Keep receipts!

Rent – this category is where you deduct rent paid for space to host a class or event. If you have a retail space you pay rent for or you pay for a space at a vendor fair or trade show, that can go here as well. This is NOT where you write off rent for any space in your home. Keep invoices or receipts!

Telephone – this is where you write off your cell phone bill. If you are working the business but not earning much, you might consider only taking a 50% deduction here. If you are all in and bringing in a good bit of revenue, then you can discuss taking 100% of your line with your tax professional. If you have a shared family plan, make sure your line is the primary line in order to maximize the deduction. For example, I have a shared plan that has my number, my son's phone line, and my iPad. I deduct 100% of my phone line as I use my phone almost exclusively for business. The plan is about $100 per month including the shared minute package and the data plan. I deduct 100% of my iPad as I purchased it so I can work remotely when I travel without having to drag my laptop everywhere. I do not deduct my son's line, which is not business related. However, if my son's line (which is $9.99 per month plus taxes and the $30 data plan) were the primary line, I would be limiting my deduction. Keep your monthly bill that shows the breakdown by number! You do not have to keep all the detailed call pages.

Chapter 14

Tricky Situations

This is the chapter you really want to read. Maybe even memorize!

This chapter covers more expenses and the same IRS guidelines apply. I am making a special point to talk about them separately and more in depth with you because these are the most difficult areas for most people to understand or they are areas that result in the IRS thinking you were out to cheat the system. Just because you need to use extra discernment with some expenses doesn't mean you shouldn't take full advantage of any legitimate deduction you have. It simply means that sometimes, we need to take extra care in how we document our expenses to make sure they hold up in the event of an audit. It also means, we want to be sure we only claim the amount we are legally entitled to claim so we don't break any tax laws and so we don't bring extra scrutiny from the IRS to all essential oil distributors.

Childcare – Childcare for your own child is never deductible as a business expense.

But what if I had to pay someone to stay with my kids for three hours while I hosted a class on essential oils?

You cannot deduct the cost of childcare on Schedule C as a business expense (or on partnership or corporate returns). You can include that cost on Form 2441 for child and dependent care expenses for purposes of calculating the childcare credit. You need to keep a receipt of how much you paid and you need to have the person who provided the care give you their name, address, and social security number. You will need this information to properly complete the Form 2441.

Now for the tricky part of the childcare situation.

If you host a class and in order to boost attendance, you offer to have on-site childcare, you can deduct the cost of this care as a business expense. I do not recommend calling it childcare on your tax return however. I would include this cost as part of Class Materials or if this class is open only to members of your downline, perhaps in Team Development (more on this to follow).

Clothing – I am frequently asked if clothing is deductible. The short answer is NO.

What about if I am attending awards night at convention and I need a formal gown/suit? I would never buy/wear that gown/suit anywhere else or for any other purpose.

The answer is still NO.

What about just attending convention in general? The dress code is business casual, but since I work from home, I mostly wear jeans and a t-shirt.

The answer is still NO.

IRS Publication 17 states that clothing can be deducted IF a) you must wear them as a condition of your employment and b) the clothes aren't suitable for every day wear.

Some of you are preparing to debate this, especially with regards to the evening gown/suit for awards night. The same publication discusses at length that it isn't enough that the clothes aren't worn outside work. It is that they can be. In the eyes of the IRS you can wear that gown/suit to weddings, parties, or other formal gatherings.

What if it is my uniform?

As an essential oil distributor, you are not required to wear a uniform. The IRS has a very narrow definition of "required as a condition of your employment." In fact, per Publication 17, "work clothing consisting of white cap, white shirt or white jacket, white bib overalls, and standard work shoes, which a painter is required by his union to wear on the job, isn't distinctive in character or in the nature of a uniform. Similarly, the costs of buying and maintaining blue work clothes worn by a welder at the request of a foreman aren't deductible." Let's not push our luck by taking deductions we aren't entitled to and will never be able to defend as the IRS is very clear about what is and is not allowed with regard to clothing deductions.

Now for the tricky part of the clothing situation.

What about branded clothing? I bought all the company branded oily gear I could get my hands on and I wear it everywhere I go to advertise my business.

While I absolutely do not recommend this, some people deduct the cost of these items under advertising. If you choose to do this, document, document, document. Keep receipts. Take pictures in this clothing at every event you attend, every class you teach, etc. In all honesty, depending on your records and your auditor, this is still not likely to hold up to scrutiny if you are audited.

Contract Labor – We are going to jump right into the tricky part of this situation. One of the fastest ways to end up in a hot bowl of alphabet soup is to break the payroll rules. The IRS, DOL, and your state have very specific rules about what they consider to be contract labor or independent contractors' vs. employees. It matters to you because if you pay someone as contract labor, you don't withhold taxes. You don't match taxes. You don't have regular payroll reporting requirements. You aren't required to pay federal or state unemployment taxes. Now you see why this is a BIG DEAL to the taxing authorities.

The IRS has excellent guidance on this and it is probably some of the clearest guidance they offer. I am including the link to the IRS guidance here for your convenience.

https://www.irs.gov/businesses/small-businesses-self-employed/independent-contractor-self-employed-or-employee

Per the IRS, "You are not an independent contractor if you perform services that can be controlled by an employer (what will be done and how it will be done). This applies even if you are given freedom of action. What matters is that the employer has the legal right to control the details of how the services are performed."

While I really hate to burst your bubble, in most of the situations I see, most of you are not hiring contract labor. I really encourage you to read up on the IRS guidance here to be certain you treat the people you are hiring according to the appropriate classification per the IRS. The penalties for misclassification can be massive. Another trick to figure out the classification of a person you are hiring is to call your state labor department. You can simply say you are thinking about starting a business and hiring someone to do (describe the work) this job on these days or for however many hours a week. Let the person on the phone know you are looking to classify the person you hire correctly as independent contractor or employee. They will usually tell you the opinion of the state. Get their name and if they have an ID number take that down as well. Make note of the date, time, person you spoke with, and what they advised on your calendar.

If you do hire someone and pay them as an independent contractor, you will need them to complete Form W-9, which you can find on the IRS website. You will need to keep copies of invoices they provide to you for payment as well as copies of cancelled checks when you pay them. If you pay any one person $600 or more in a single calendar year, you are required to issue them a Form 1099 MISC and file both the Form 1099 MISC and Form 1096 with the IRS in January of the following year.

Employees – Much like with Contract Labor, we are going to jump write into the tricky situation here. You can use the same link I provided above under Contract Labor to access the IRS guidance on employees. Here is the IRS definition: "Under common-law rules, anyone who performs services for you is your employee *if you can control what will be done and how it will be done.* This is so even when you give the employee freedom of action. What matters is that you have the right to control the details of how the services are performed."

Example 1: You hire me to prepare your income tax return. I obtain your information and go prepare the return. I provide you with a draft to review, make any necessary adjustments, file your return, and provide you with a copy. I am an independent contractor. You have no say in any of the work or how it is performed.

Example 2: You hire a college student to come in twice a month and sit at your computer to enter all your income and expense transactions into your software program and mail out any packages you may have. You tell the student what hours they will work, where they will perform the work, and you have them enter the information per your instructions. The student is your employee. You tell them when, where, and how to perform the work.

When you hire an employee, you must have them complete Form W-4 which you can find on the IRS website. You will need them to keep a time sheet. You will be responsible for withholding federal and state income taxes, social security, and Medicare. You will also be responsible for matching social security and Medicare. In addition, you will be required to file quarterly payroll reports for both federal and state and pay unemployment taxes. You will also be required to issue your employee a Form W2 and file a copy of the Form W2 and Form W3 with the Social Security Administration in January of the following year. In some states, you are required to have Worker's Compensation insurance as well.

I recommend you hire a payroll company or professional who provides this service. Payroll penalties are steep and even making a deposit one day late can result in severe penalties.

Home Office – This is one of the biggest benefits of having your own business, at least in terms of taxes. Think about it. Whether you have a business or not, you already pay rent or mortgage payments and utilities. Now, you might qualify for a tax deduction.

There are many tax professionals that say claiming the business use of home deduction increases your chance of being audited. I have never seen this to be the case. I think as with any other deduction, claiming an obscene percentage of expenses may increase your risk, so just be accurate and reasonable!

In Publication 587, the IRS states "to qualify to deduct expenses for business use of your home, you must use part of your home exclusively and regularly as your principal place of business. The area used for business can be a room or other separately identifiable space."

What does this mean? This means you can measure off any separately used space that is exclusively for business to include that measurement in your space

76

used for business. I office at home and I have my entire dining room that is used exclusively for business. My dining room is 8 ft by 10 ft. Additionally, I have 3 business file cabinets in a closet and the space they use is 4 ft by 2 ft. I have several boxes of archived files that have yet to be scanned in and the space they take up is 6 ft by 3 ft. My total business use space is 106 sq ft. If my total square footage is 700 sq ft. My business use space is 15.14%. I am not limited to the 80 square feet of the dining room. I am allowed the additional 26 feet of space used exclusively for business as well.

For business use of home, you fill out Form 8829 if you are filing Schedule C. Your expenses will almost all go in the indirect expense column. The exception will usually be repairs and maintenance, such as painting or carpet specifically for the space you are claiming exclusively for business. You can include mortgage interest and property taxes or rent if you do not own your home. If you do own your home and also pay PMI, you can include that as well. You can include home owner's insurance or renter's insurance. You can include your utilities, repairs and maintenance, housekeeping, HOA dues, landscaping, pest control, and security. Keep invoices and statements! Take pictures of your exclusive use spaces!

The tricky part of the home office situation is what constitutes exclusive use.

Now, the word exclusive seems pretty clear to me, but I see clients who want to write off half their entry way or a portion of their living room and kitchen because they host classes. Do not be tempted to do this. You are already getting to deduct a portion of your regular life expenses that you wouldn't be able to deduct if you just had a plain old job.

Mixed Use Assets – these are assets that can be used for both business and personal. This entire category is a tricky situation. Some of these items are more tricky than others though.

Cell Phone – if you truly work your business, you can buy a new cell phone and it can be deducted. This means YOUR cell phone, not the one you buy for yourself and then the one you buy for your son or daughter three months later.

Computer – if you are working the business, you can write off the cost of your computer / printer you purchase to use for business. You can even give your old computer to your kids. You cannot write off 100% of a new computer if you use it half the time for business and your kids use it half the time. Then you can only write off 50%. If or when you can afford to, I recommend having your own computer for your business that your children don't have access to.

iPad – this is the same as for the computer and printer.

The trickiest of these are the items I am often asked about that can be used every day in the kitchen. I have been asked about blenders, margarita machines, and Kitchen Aid mixers. If you choose to write off any portion of any cost of any of these items, I would do so sparingly and document, document, document. Notice I did not say don't do it. If you host 5 classes/events per month and use your margarita machine to make lavender lemonade, I would absolutely take a deduction for a percentage of that margarita machine. I would not take more than 50% because it is just too easy for the IRS to argue it was really for your backyard barbeque. I would take photos of every event making sure to capture the margarita machine and even people dispensing drinks from it. On the other hand, if you use the margarita machine for one class/event per year, I would not take the risk.

The same goes for blenders such as a Vitamix that can be used to make frozen drinks or smoothies and mixers that can be used to make body butters and lotions as well as desserts for classes. Keep your receipts!

Oil Purchases – Be prepared for some wordiness here! Oil purchases aren't really tricky. Much like the home office exclusive use rule, Internal Revenue Code Section 262 specifically states the following: "Except as otherwise expressly stated in this chapter, no deduction shall be allowed for personal, living, or family expenses." The only thing they have expressly stated thereafter is with regards to land line telephone expenses.

What does this mean?

This means you cannot deduct any oils you use for personal use.

What about my 100 PV I have to spend to get my commission though? I am required to spend that to get paid so it is definitely a tax deductible business expense.

It is not. I have this conversation over and over with people and I have found the easiest way to explain it is this: Let's say you spend 100 PV. Your order consists of one bottle each of lemon, lavender, and peppermint for an oil class, one bottle of lime for

80

your personal Cinco de Mayo celebration, and two bottles of shampoo for your family. Your commission is $57. As a prudent business person, should you have spent $100 to make $57? Of course not, and you didn't. You spent $30 to make $57 and then you spent $70 on personal items.

Now, let's say instead you bought 10 bottles of peppermint oil for 100PV to send out as promos for anyone who joins during the month. Your 100PV is deductible in this scenario as long as you really do give away the 10 bottles of peppermint oil.

So, hopefully now you understand why you cannot just write off the 100PV per month. Let's talk about how to classify your oil purchases that you can write off.

One way, probably the easiest way, is to deduct the total spent on business purchases on the Cost of Goods Sold line. The problem is when the IRS sees Cost of Goods Sold, they also expect to see inventory and unless you have a retail sales venue, you don't have inventory.

You can just add a line called Oil Purchases under Other Expenses. I do not recommend this though. If you do this and Oil Purchases is disproportionately larger than any of your other expense categories, you are more likely to be audited.

So what can you do?

I recommend the following:

1) When you receive any order, immediately highlight or mark in some obvious way which purchases are business and which purchases are personal.

2) Write which category you are including them in on the packing list that comes with them.

3) Save this page in your files or scan and save it to your computer.

Oil purchase categories:

Class Materials – this should be any oil or product you order for use specifically in a class. Maybe you go through two kits a year letting everyone sample the oils. Maybe you like to prepare peppermint brownies for every class. Whatever oils you are using specifically for a class, put them here.

Demo Products – I have heard many people say they have been told they can write off first time use products. The answer is sort of. You can't write it off just because you have never tried it before. You can write it off if you have never tried it before, but you are letting everyone else try it or if you are ordering the products so everyone can see them. For example, each year at convention, new products are announced. You purchase all of them so you can take them home and demonstrate all these new products for your team. These are all first time purchases. You can use them, but your team is also using them. I like to think of these products as your everyday testers that are on display in the stores.

Promos and Samples – these are products you give away. You either order the bottle specifically to give out samples to certain people or groups of people or you are running a promotion that is open to anyone. For example, I have a colleague who suffers from migraines. I ordered a bottle of oil specifically so she could try it. I don't have migraines so I will never use that oil. I would include it here. Maybe in the fall I decide to run a promotion and I will give away a bottle of cinnamon oil to every new member that signs up. That is a promo and the cost of all those bottles of cinnamon oil go here.

Team Development – I saved this one for last because this is part of our next tricky situation. Many distributors send out oils to members of their downlines. They offer incentives for team members if they accomplish certain metrics during the month or the quarter. Let's say I decide that for every person in my downline who adds 100 new members in the year I am going to send them a bottle of Sandalwood oil. The cost of the Sandalwood goes here. Why here and not promos? Promos are open to everyone. Team Development is for members of your team only. Why here and not Gifts? The gift limit is $25. Gifts should be reserved for special occasions. This incentive is not a gift. It is a business strategy to grow and develop your team.

You have now taken one of your largest expense categories and broken it down into four separate categories. Not only does this look better on your tax return, it also allows you to see what specific area you are spending the most money on and adjust your spending and efforts according to which area is bringing you the best return on those dollars.

Continuing with Team Development, this is also where you deduct all things to do with team building. Maybe you bought three extra tickets to convention and you will use those to take your strongest builders or maybe those who are struggling with being all in so they can get just a taste of what it's like to be a part of this special industry. Those tickets go here! Product credits, team meetings, rank up rewards, and anything else you do to incentivize your downline to grow and further develop your team goes here. Many of you give a resource guide to new members because how else will they learn all the great things about their oils? Those can go here! I recommend to most of my clients instead of giving builders on your team oils or even product credits for oils, give them business development materials such as this book or other business development related books. Give them a ticket to a conference or seminar on network marketing or just entrepreneurial business in general. Keep receipts for whatever you do and document who you gave what and why on your calendar!

Travel – You may be asking why I chose to put travel in the tricky situation chapter. Not all travel is tricky. You fly to convention by yourself and stay in a hotel. Nothing tricky about that. 100 percent of the cost is a tax write off.

You fly to convention with your spouse who has a full time job and you stay in a hotel. Your flight and the hotel are deductible. Your portion of the meals is deductible. The flight and meals for your spouse is not deductible.

You fly to convention with your spouse who works the business with you and you stay in a hotel. All your costs are tax deductible.

You travel to teach a class in your hometown, 1300 miles away. You are gone 6 days. You teach one class and spend the rest of the time with family and friends. You scheduled the trip to be there for a friend's wedding and just happened to end up having a class. Your travel is not deductible.

Let's say you know your friend is going to get married on a certain Saturday in October in your home town 1300 miles away. You work with family members, friends, maybe even other downline members and schedule two classes before the wedding (Wednesday and Thursday). You return home on Sunday. You are gone 5 days. Since two of the five days are for business, you can deduct 40% of the travel costs (airfare or mileage), hotel only for those two days, meals only for those two days plus 40% of the meals getting there and back.

Let's say you know your friend is going to get married on a certain Saturday in October in your home town 1300 miles away. You work with family members, friends, maybe even other downline members and schedule two classes before the wedding (Thursday and Friday) and one class the Monday after the wedding. Now your full trip is deductible because your business carries past the weekend and it is more cost effective to stay the weekend then travel home and back.

Keep all your travel receipts. Document your classes. Keep your sign in sheets. Take pictures of the classes. I recommend emailing people to schedule the classes BEFORE you book your flight. This further legitimizes the business purpose aspect.

I know the last thing in this section you really want to know is what about the cost of traveling with your kids. Much like childcare, you cannot deduct the cost of travel for your children. What if they work for you and you pay them? The answer is still no. Unless your child is 16 or older and can have their own account, you cannot justify to the IRS your child had a business purpose for traveling.

Chapter 15

Closing Anecdotes

I know. I know. This book has been so fun to read you really want more!

The tax code is so vague in most places it is difficult to write a book that covers every situation. The first thing to remember is the IRS will always side in favor of the government and "ordinary and necessary" is at the discretion of your auditor. This might be how I passed a tax class or two!

In all seriousness though, this example was given when I was in my first month or so of training with the IRS. A heart surgeon in Oklahoma City makes a $1,000,000 a year. He purchases a car that cost $100,000. The doctor is self-employed. Can he write off the business use of his car using actual expenses?

This question was asked of 50 new revenue agents. I was the only one that said yes. I gained the immediate attention of the entire class, and the instructor asked a few people why they said no before asking me why I said yes. All those who said no did so saying the cost of $100,000 car is not necessary. I gave an example that the average person makes $50,000 to $75,000 per year and buys a car that costs $30,000 which is nearly half their annual income. The doctor's car was only a tenth of his annual income, so in his profession, it was in fact ordinary. I mean, who wants the heart surgeon who can only afford a $30,000 Prius?

I was correct. However, we all passed the class. The point is, most IRS auditors have never owned a business. They have always collected a paycheck from someone else. What you and I deem "ordinary and necessary" will not compute for many of them. Documenting everything as I have suggested though will definitely give you the advantage if you are ever selected for audit.

Sometimes, your auditor is human. I once audited a man who worked for an elevator company. They were required to wear a uniform that consisted of the company shirt and green pants. Now, technically, those green pants do not meet the definition of a uniform that cannot be worn anywhere else. However, I could not fathom anyone WOULD wear so hideous pants in public for any reason other than they had to so I let him keep the deduction. Don't assume you will be that lucky. And again, this example goes to show the discretion lies with the auditor!

For additional resources, please check my website:

www.whatcanideductbook.com

for links to IRS guidance on various small business topics, a Sample Log template covered in Chapter 5, and even an Excel spreadsheet template if you are using the Excel method covered in Chapter 8.

This is also where you can purchase additional copies of this book!

Some of you are looking for a bit more tax related information or maybe even business structure guidance. I have not covered complex tax strategies in this book or even when, how, or why you might consider a S-corp structure vs. a sole-proprietorship because I think everyone needs a good solid resource for the basics first.

If you are at a point in your business where you are ready for a different structure or more complex tax strategies, please contact your tax professional. If you do not have a tax professional, or your tax professional is not familiar with direct selling businesses, you are welcome to reach out to me.

Dee Dee Stone
Number Crunchers
www.deedeestone.com

Check back at www.whatcanideductbook.com for future books on more complex strategies and live seminars in your area.

APPENDIX A

Sample Chart of Accounts

Commission Income
Other Income

Advertising
Automobile
Bank Charges
Bulk Buy Purchases
Class Materials
Computer and Internet
Contract Labor
Demo Products
Dues and Subscriptions
Gifts
Home Office
Interest Expense
Legal and Professional Fees
Maintenance Fees
Meals and Entertainment
Merchant Account Fees
Office Furniture and Equipment
Office Expenses
Payroll Taxes
Postage
Professional Development

Promos and Samples

Rent

Team Development

Telephone

Travel

Wages